The Elizabethan
Religious Settlement

by

Claire Cross

HEADSTART HISTORY

Published by	HEADSTART HISTORY PO Box 41, Bangor, Gwynedd, LL57 1SB
Set by	C.B.S. 155 Hamilton Road, Felixstowe, Suffolk, IP11 7DR
Printed by	Henry Ling Ltd., The Dorset Press, Dorchester.
ISBN	1 873041 60 8

A CIP catalogue record for this book is available from the British Library.

CONTENTS

N.B.

With one or two exceptions footnotes have only been given to original sources; the secondary sources upon which this essay has relied are discussed in *Further Reading*.

INTRODUCTION

The HEADSTART HISTORY PAPERS aim to identify important themes and topics the significance of which extends beyond the studies of professional historians. The PAPERS are distillations of the research of distinguished scholars in a form appropriate to students and the general reader.

The settlement of religion was, as Claire Cross points out, one of the most urgent problems confronting the young Elizabeth. As Anne Boleyn's daughter she was almost a living symbol of the break with Rome. She had lived through the protestantism of her brother Edward VI and survived the threats and dangers of the catholicism of her sister Mary I. On her accession Elizabeth indicated her intention to return to the policies of her father and brother and that choice was underlined by her appointment of William Cecil as Principal Secretary and we should not underestimate the importance of his role as an intermediary between the queen and her first archbishop, Matthew Parker. Parker was always uneasy of the queen and her church as well as Cecil's support for the royal supremacy and uniformity. However, it was largely through the efforts of Elizabeth and Cecil that the religious settlement survived until the Civil War.

Few are as well qualified as Claire Cross to write on Elizabeth's religious settlement. He early research was carried out under the supervision of Geoffrey Elton and led to her first important book on Henry Hastings, third Earl of Huntingdon. Many students have been led through the intricacies of the sixteenth century church by her *Church and People 1450-1660* first published by Fontana in 1976. The bibliography demonstrates her research interests and we note in particular her work on York where she is Professor of History.

Claire Cross has been a firm supporter of HEADSTART HIS-TORY since the publication of its first book, MONASTIC STUDIES in 1990. It is a pleasure to thank her for that support for making an important contribution to this series.

Judith Loades
Bangor 1992

Precisely three days after Mary Tudor died, on 20 November 1558 Elizabeth I appointed William Cecil her principal secretary. 'I give you this charge that you shall be of my Privy Council and content to take pains for me and my realm,' she is reported to have said to her new minister, adding 'This judgement I have of you that you will not be corrupted by any manner of gift and that you will be faithful to the state; and that without respect of my private will you will give me that counsel which you think best...'[1] By choosing Cecil as her chief adviser so soon after she came to the throne Elizabeth signalled her intention to return to the policies of her father and her brother. In the short term Cecil probably contributed more than any other councillor to achieving the parliamentary settlement of religion in 1559. As the intermediary between the queen and her first archbishop of Canterbury, Matthew Parker, he played an equally major role in the implementation of the Acts of Supremacy and Uniformity which in the long term converted England into a protestant nation.

I Antecedents

The Acts of Supremacy and Uniformity, the constituent parts of the Elizabethan settlement, originated in legislation passed in the Henrician and Edwardian periods, the Act of Supremacy having a considerably longer pedigree, as the Church of England became a national church a good two decades before it gained an unequivocally protestant liturgy. The break with Rome took several years to effect in the reign

1 Quoted in C. Read, *Mr Secretary Cecil and Queen Elizabeth* (London, 1955), p. 119.

of Henry VIII and, at least in its early stages, the king kept the changes reversible in case the pope should succumb and grant the annulment of his marriage to Katherine of Aragon. In the first session of the Reformation Parliament the crown encouraged the Commons merely to mount a general attack on the covetousness of the clergy, but in the ensuing years went on to address the problem of papal authority directly. The Submission of the Clergy in 1532 marked a crucial stage along this path. Subjects of the pope no longer, the brow beaten clergy in this capitulation conceded that they owed allegiance to the king alone. The 1533 Act in Restraint of Appeals, citing 'sundry old authentic histories and chronicles', proclaimed the inherent unity of the English state.

> 'This realm of England is an empire, and so hath been accepted in the world, governed by one supreme head and king, having the dignity and royal estate of the imperial crown of the same, unto whom a body politic, compact of all sorts and degrees of people divided in terms and by names of spirituality and temporalty, be bounden and owe to bear next to God a natural and humble obedience...'[2]

The ensuing 1534 Act of Supremacy completed the process. After recognising that the crown had always rightfully possessed powers over the church as well as the state, it laid down 'that the king our sovereign lord, his heirs and successors, kings of this realm, shall be taken, accepted and reputed the only supreme head in earth of the Church of

2 G. R. Elton, *The Tudor Constitution* (Cambridge, 1960), p. 344.

England...'[3]

Regarding himself as a second Constantine Henry VIII henceforth never deviated from his belief in the royal supremacy, but remained ambiguous in his attitude towards religious reform. So long as Cromwell held the reins of power, in 1535 he permitted the dissemination of an English translation of the bible and sanctioned the expression of mildly evangelical beliefs in the Ten Articles of 1536, only to insist in the 1539 Act of Six Articles upon a reaffirmation of the central catholic doctrine of transubstantiation and traditional catholic practices such as clerical celibacy, private masses, auricular confession and, for the laity, communion in one kind. By royal command from 1544 all churches used Cranmer's translation of the litany into English, but that apart, the old Latin liturgy, shorn of references to the bishop of Rome, continued in force until the king's death.

On the accession of Edward VI and Protector Somerset's assumption of power the English Reformation moved into its second phase. Throughout the reign of Henry VIII Thomas Cranmer, archbishop of Canterbury since 1532, had conformed his will to the will of the supreme governor. Personally much more sympathetic to religious change Somerset allowed the archbishop freedom to advance protestant ideas, and Cranmer took the opportunity to bring to England continental protestant leaders like Martin Bucer and Peter Martyr driven from the empire after the victory in 1547 of Charles V over the protestant princes at Mühlberg. Under Cranmer's direction a commission of English clerics

3 *op. cit.*, p. 355.

in 1549 produced 'the Book of the Common Prayer and administration of the sacraments and other rites and ceremonies of the church after the use of the Church of England' which Parliament in the first Act of Uniformity ordered all ministers to adopt 'from and after the feast of Pentecost next coming.'[4] Now for the first time the English church possessed a liturgy entirely in English, and the English laity might receive at communion the wine as well as the bread, but the new Prayer Book, chiefly derived from the Latin missal, still appeared conservative in its theology.

It was at this point in the English Reformation, with the church separated from Rome but as yet without a decisively protestant liturgy, that the one man who more than any other can be regarded as the architect of the Elizabethan settlement emerged on the political scene. When Henry VIII had established his supremacy over the English church William Cecil had been a pupil of the humanist John Cheke at St John's College, Cambridge. At the university he had enthusiastically supported the 'new learning', even progressing in his relatively short academic career to teach Greek to some of the junior members of his college. Immediately before his departure from Cambridge to study law in London in 1541 he married his tutor's sister, Mary Cheke, and then, after her premature death, in 1543 took as his second wife, Mildred, one of the five learned daughters of Sir Anthony Cooke. Both these alliances linked him with a circle consciously working for religious reform. Even though through his father, a yeoman of the Wardrobe, and Cheke, from 1544 tutor to Prince Edward, he had entry to the court, he never gained office under the old king.

4 *op. cit.*, pp. 393-4.

The accession of Edward VI saw the beginning of Cecil's public career; in 1547 Somerset appointed him his private secretary and in 1550 he obtained what at first must have seemed a rather minor position, that of surveyor of the estates of the Princess Elizabeth. In that same year he became one of the two secretaries of state, in almost continuous attendance upon the Privy Council. As secretary of the Council Cecil found himself called upon to advance protestantism in England, first as a member of the 1551 commission to revise ecclesiastical laws, then, indirectly, but even more importantly in the undertaking which resulted in the second Edwardian Prayer Book.

The archbishop and his fellow protestant bishops had for some time felt uneasy over the conservatism of the first Prayer Book, and when he went on to revise it Cranmer had sought the advice of Bucer, Martyr and other continental theologians. Probably as a preliminary to the imposition of the second Prayer Book in November 1551 Cecil chaired at his house in London a private conference on the Lord's Supper at which Sir John Cheke and the theologians Robert Horne, David Whitehead and Edmund Grindal contested the protestant interpretation of the eucharist against the conservatives John Feckenham, John Young and Thomas Watson. In April 1552 Parliament passed the second Act of Uniformity which enforced the second Edwardian Prayer Book upon the church from 1 November following.

Unlike the 1549 Prayer Book the second Prayer Book of Edward VI made no concessions whatsoever. Whereas opaque phrases in the first Prayer Book had permitted catholics still to look upon the sacrament of holy communion

6

as a perpetual sacrifice for the living and the dead, now, with communion tables replacing stone altars, the new book laid emphasis upon the sacrament as a commemoration of the Last Supper and a service of thanksgiving. The black rubric, which the Privy Council added to the Book after it had been completed by the commission of divines, went to some lengths to explain that kneeling at communion implied no adoration of the sacred elements. On the promulgation of this liturgy the Church of England, until then a church in schism from Rome, became a quite explicitly protestant church.

The death of Edward VI little more than six months after the imposition of the second Act of Uniformity meant that the nation at large had only a brief experience of the 1552 Prayer Book before the next monarch, Mary Tudor, encouraged the resumption of catholic practice. In the autumn of 1553 Mary's first Parliament enacted that

> 'all such divine service and administration of sacraments as were most commonly used in the realm of England in the last year of the reign of our late sovereign lord King Henry the Eighth shall be, from and after the 20th day of December in this present year of our Lord God 1553, used and frequented through the whole realm of England and all other the Queen's Majesty's dominions.'[5]

Mary found it much easier to restore catholic ritual than to divest herself of the royal supremacy, and again she had no

5 *op. cit.*, p. 400.

choice but to employ Parliament. Only after the pope had confirmed lay owners in their possession of former monastic lands did Parliament agree to seek a formal reconciliation between England and the holy see and pass an act to 'repeal and abrogate such acts and statutes as had been made in Parliament since the said 20th year of the said King Henry the Eighth against the supremacy of the see Apostolic.'[6]

Implicated in Northumberland's attempt to divert the succession in favour of Lady Jane Grey, Cecil withdrew from the Council after Mary's accession. Although several of his friends and kindred, including his father-in-law, Sir Anthony Cooke, chose to go to the continent on account of their religion, he conformed and lived most of the reign in retirement, surfacing only to sit in Mary's fourth Parliament which rejected a bill designed to confiscate the property of exiles who refused to return to their native land. He continued, however, to oversee the administration of Princess Elizabeth's estates. As it became obvious in the last eighteen months of her life that the queen would never bear a child, his connection with the heir presumptive assumed a new importance. Early in November 1558 Mary at last agreed to recognise her half-sister as her successor, and in consequence Elizabeth had the opportunity to plan her accession at least a fortnight in advance.

II The Settlement

The settlement of religion was one of the most urgent problems confronting the new queen. Theoretically Eliza-

6 *op. cit.*, pp. 360.

beth could have kept her realm in the Roman obedience. Philip II of Spain, to retain England in the Habsburg interest, offered to marry his former sister-in-law, and had this happened the papacy would doubtless have recognised Elizabeth as the de facto queen. Elizabeth, however, because of the circumstances of her birth, her father having married Anne Boleyn during the life time of Katherine of Aragon, may have considered that she had no alternative but to sever the country from Rome for the second time in the century. Her selection of Cecil as her principal secretary at her first Council meeting on 20 November 1558 demonstrated that she had already decided to make a break with her sister's regime, and probably also determined the outcome of the settlement. On the very day the Privy Council met for the first time, William Bill, summoned from retirement by Cecil, delivered a protestant sermon at Paul's Cross in London. When the following week the bishop of Winchester publicly accused Bill of heresy, the Privy Council retaliated by sending Christopherson to prison. Elizabeth demonstrated her rejection of the doctrine of transubstantiation and gave a further indication of the direction her government would take by walking out of mass when the celebrant attempted to elevate the sacred elements at Christmas 1558.

The queen retained some Marian councillors like William Paulet, Marquis of Winchester, in her new Privy Council, but the inner core of councillors which coalesced around Cecil showed a quite clear protestant alignment. Nicholas Bacon, like Cecil married to a daughter of Sir Anthony Cooke, had taken refuge on the continent on account of his religion in the previous reign. The queen's cousin, Sir Francis Knollys, had also gone into exile, as had Francis

Russell, the new Earl of Bedford. Also like Cecil, most of these councillors had already had considerable experience of government under Edward VI. Rather than seek an entirely new compromise when devising the Elizabethan settlement, the queen and her councillors turned for guidance to parallel developments in the Edwardian period. A disproportionate number of vacancies had occurred on the episcopal bench in the last few months of Mary's reign, and the Archbishop of Canterbury, Reginald Cardinal Pole, died on the same day as the queen herself; consequently the new government could immediately begin making arrangements to fill the empty sees. Once again the soundings being made in the first few weeks of the reign furnish further proof of the regime's commitment to protestantism. On 9 December 1558 Sir Nicholas Bacon wrote to Matthew Parker, once a fellow student at Corpus Christi College, Cambridge, concerning 'certain matters touching yourself, which I trust shall turn you to good.' Later that month Cecil ordered Parker to come immediately to London, 'the queen's highness, minding presently to use your service in certain matters of importance.'[7] So early had the queen's advisers begun planning the new religious settlement, but as long as England remained officially in communion with Rome no formal appointments could yet be made. Because of the precedents set in the reigns of Henry VIII, Edward VI and Mary only Parliament could formally sanction a change in religion.

Scarcely two months after her accession, Elizabeth's first

7 J. Bruce and T. T. Perowne, eds., *Correspondence of Matthew Parker* (Parker Society, Cambridge, 1853), pp. 49, 53.

Parliament assembled in Westminster on 25 January 1559. Although the House contained some convinced catholics, from the outset most of the Commons seem to have been willing to follow the queen in rejecting the papacy. The Lords, in contrast, proved far less conciliatory. Despite the thinning of their ranks through epidemics in the previous few months, twenty of the Lords Spiritual survived to assume their seats and, to the government's consternation, virtually all expressed their allegiance to the pope. Convocation, the representative body of the clergy, which customarily sat along side Parliament, adopted as equally emphatic stance against any alteration in religion. This left the councillors in little doubt that, were they to persist in plans for a second breach with Rome, they would have to face resistance from most of the higher clergy. Despite the probability of substantial opposition, religious change came to the fore early in the session. At the beginning of February 1559 the Commons read a Supremacy Bill, and later that month approved a Bill combining both Supremacy and religious Uniformity only for the Bill to founder in the Upper House. A majority of members of the Lords could grudgingly countenance the queen's assumption of the title of supreme head of the English church, but objected to giving any formal recognition to protestantism. They furthermore refused to repeal the heresy laws which had made possible the persecution of protestants under Mary. The protestants in the Commons, greatly perturbed by this turn of events, then introduced a new bill which would have permitted all who so wished to practice without penalty the form of religion in force in the last year of Edward VI's reign.

The government originally appears to have planned to

dissolve Parliament before Easter, which fell on 26 March in 1559. All it could now hope to achieve before that date was an emasculated Act of Supremacy without an Act of Uniformity. This would have left the country in a very divided state, with protestants in London and some forward areas taking the law into their own hands, while the majority of the nation continued to observe the catholic mass. Then at the eleventh hour the queen determined not to dissolve Parliament and issued a proclamation enabling the laity to receive communion in both kinds at Easter.

This decision may have been brought about by the improvement in the international situation which lessened the government's apprehension of catholic opposition within England. Elizabeth had inherited a country at war with France and in alliance with Spain. Because of the rivalry between the Habsburgs and the Valois she could still rely on the tacit support of Philip II, but to order her affairs freely at home she desperately needed peace with France, a matter made all the more urgent because of the renewal of the old alliance between Scotland and France. Mary Queen of Scots, the catholic claimant to the English throne, was married to the dauphin of France and an invasion of England through Scotland remained a very real possibility, particularly since Cecil had been sending English aid to the rebellious protestant Scots Lords of the Congregation. Negotiations begun with France in February 1559 did much to reduce the tension: by Easter the queen knew that only her reluctance to acknowledge the loss of Calais prevented the conclusion of a treaty. It now seemed unlikely that either the French or the Spanish would risk prejudicing the peace. Freed from fears of foreign intervention the queen consequently could concentrate upon trying to obtain a religious settlement.

At this juncture Cecil may well have recalled the theological discussions over which he had presided in the Edwardian period. To discredit the catholic bishops the Privy Council arranged for a disputation to take place in Holy week in Westminster Abbey. The propositions for debate - that the word of God did not permit the mass to be regarded as a sacrifice for the living and the dead, or the liturgy to be offered in a tongue inaccessible to the people; and that every national church had a right to change its ceremonies so long as they made for edification - exhibited a clear protestant bias. The proceedings, in themselves inconclusive, gave the government a pretext for claiming that the catholic theologians had been vanquished. The disruptive behaviour of two of the catholic disputants, Bishops Watson and White, in addition provided an excuse for imprisoning them in the Tower and depleted the catholic resistance in the Lords yet further.

When Parliament reconvened after Easter the government renewed its attempt to achieve a settlement of religion, this time introducing separate bills for Supremacy and Uniformity, so that even if the Uniformity Bill failed, the break with Rome could be secured. Catholics found the idea of a woman being head of the church doubly offensive, while protestants also had scruples on the matter. As early as December 1558, before his return from exile, Thomas Sampson, who believed 'all scripture seems to assign the title of head of the church to Christ alone', had been asking Peter Martyr for advice on, 'how ought we to act with respect to allowing or disallowing the title of "after Christ supreme head of the Church of England"?'[8] The new bill partially met this difficulty by altering the queen's style. After rehearsing how in the reign of Henry VIII 'divers good laws and statutes were made and established, as well for the utter extinguishment and putting away of all usurped and foreign powers and authorities out of this your realm..., as also for the restoring and uniting to the imperial crown of this realm the ancient jurisdictions, authorities, superiorities and preeminences to the same of right belonging and appertaining...' it went on to acknowledge that

> 'the queen's highness is the only supreme governor of this realm and of all her highness' dominions and countries, as well in all spiritual or ecclesiastical things or causes as temporal, and that no foreign prince, person, prelate, state or potentate hath or ought to have any jurisdiction, power, superiority, preeminence or authority ecclesiastical or spiritual within this realm...'[9]

This bill, which also repealed the old heresy laws and authorised communion in both kinds, passed through the Commons with little dissent, but fared very differently in the Lords where Nicholas Heath, the Marian Archbishop of York, led the attack. The catholic bishops now realised, as they had not perceived in the reign of Henry VIII, that if catholicism were to be preserved in England the nation must be kept in obedience to Rome. The conservative laity, on the other hand, had not yet reached this understanding. All the

8 H. Robinson, ed., *The Zurich Letters* (Parker Society, Cambridge, 1842), p. 1.
9 Elton, *Tudor Constitution*, pp. 363, 366.

lords spiritual opposed the Supremacy Bill, but only one lord temporal voted against it; so the Bill gained the approval of the majority the House. The alteration in the queen's style had little practical effect upon her authority within the church. As John Parkhurst, another Marian exile, pointed out to Henry Bullinger at the time, 'the queen is not willing to be called the *head* of the church of England, although this title has been offered her; but she willingly accepts the title of *governor*, which amounts to the same thing.'[10] The bishops, however, did succeed in inserting into the bill a clause defining heresy solely as that which had been adjudged to be heresy by the first four councils of the church, and in so doing protected conservatives against a religious persecution by protestants in the future.

On the passing of the Act of Supremacy by both the Commons and the Lords the government had obtained half the settlement, and the crown had now to all intents and purposes been restored to the position it had enjoyed in the Henrician and Edwardian periods after the break with Rome. The Bill to enforce uniformity in religion received a much more difficult passage, as events in Parliament before Easter had indicated might well be the case. The laity in Parliament seem to have felt little loyalty for the papacy, or to have comprehended the necessity for the English catholic church to remain in communion with Rome, but, especially in the Upper House, made clear their preference for the old religion and in particular for the Latin mass. Ignoring these objections the new Act of Uniformity declared the government's intention to return to the religious situation in the last

10 *Zurich letters*, p. 29.

months of Edward VI's reign when the former 'Act for the Uniformity of Common Prayer and administration of the Sacraments' had been in force. Reciting how 'to the great decay of the due honour of God and discomfort to the professors of the truth of Christ's religion' the first Parliament of Queen Mary had repealed this Act of Uniformity, the present Parliament enacted

> that the said statute of repeal and everything therein contained... shall be void and of none effect from and after the feast of the Nativity of St John the Baptist next coming; and that the said book with the order of service and of the administration of sacraments, rites and ceremonies, with the alterations and additions therein added and appointed by this statute shall stand and be from and after the said feast...'[11]

The significant alterations and additions to the second Edwardian Prayer Book mentioned in the Bill related to the communion service. The priest when offering the bread and wine to the recipient now spoke the biblical words of institution, 'the body of our Lord Jesus Christ, which was given for thee, preserve thy body and soul into everlasting life', and 'the blood of our Lord Jesus Christ, which was shed for thee, preserve thy body and soul into everlasting life', as well as the two commemorative sayings contained in the Edwardian Book, 'Take and eat this in remembrance that Christ died for thee, and feed on him in thine heart by faith, with thanksgiving' and 'Drink this in remembrance

---

11 Elton, *Tudor Constitution*, p. 401.

that Christ's blood was shed for thee, and be thankful.'[12]
This phraseology in no sense conflicted with the teaching of
Bucer and Calvin on the true presence of Christ in the
sacrament and the returning exiles found no doctrinal state-
ments in the Prayer Book with which they could not concur.
At the time they do not seem to have paid much attention to
the clause in the Bill which, introducing the other major
deviation from the Second Edwardian Prayer Book, provided 'that such ornaments of the church and of the ministers
thereof shall be retained and be in use as was in the Church
of England by authority of Parliament in the second year of
the reign of King Edward the Sixth until other order shall be
therein taken...'[13]

With this lead given by the government, and with the support
of a small band of returned exiles with seats in the House,
which included Sir Anthony Cooke, the Act of Uniformity
gained the Commons' assent without much difficulty, but
ran into severe problems in the Lords. All the lords spiritual
who had opposed the Act of Supremacy also opposed this
bill, but now they could also count upon the support of a
sizeable number of lay lords unwilling to reject the mass.
Only twenty-one peers voted in favour of the bill with
eighteen against. Had the bishops of Lincoln and Winchester not been confined in the Tower and the Abbot of
Westminster absented himself, the bill would have failed.
Neither the Supremacy Bill nor the Bill of Uniformity

12 W. K. Clay, ed., *Liturgies and Occasional Forms of Prayer set forth in the Reign of Queen Elizabeth* (Parker Society, Cambridge, 1847), p. 195.
13 Elton, *Tudor Constitution*, p. 403.

obtained the consent of the lords spiritual or of the clergy in either house of Convocation, but this did not prevent their inclusion on the statute book. Two further bills, one dissolving the monasteries and chantries refounded by Mary, the other restoring first fruits and tenths from ecclesiastical benefices to the crown, completed the legislation which created the settlement.

The manoeuvres behind the proceedings in the first parliament of Elizabeth have given rise to much contention among historians. A protestant cleric and former exile, John Jewel, in letters to his Zurich friends from London during the parliamentary sitting went out of his way to stress the threat posed by the Marian bishops to effecting any protestant settlement. 'The bishops are a great hindrance to us', he wrote to Peter Martyr on 20 March 1559, 'for being, as you know, among the nobility and leading men in the Upper House, and having none there on our side to expose their artifices and confute their falsehoods, they reign as sole monarchs in the midst of ignorant and weak men, and easily overreach our little party, either by their numbers, or their reputation for learning.' The queen', he believed, however, 'openly favours our cause... She is... prudently, and firmly, and piously following up her purpose, though somewhat more slowly than we could wish.'[14] In his *Acts and Monuments*, which first appeared in England in 1563, John Foxe also depicted Elizabeth as a defender of protestantism against the papalists and described how, despite all the activities of the pope's champions in the Lords, 'through the merciful goodness of the Lord, the true cause of the gospel had the upper hand, the papists' hope was frustrate, and their

14 *Zurich Letters*, p. 10.

rage abated, the order and proceedings of King Edward's time concerning religion were revived again, the supremacy of the pope abolished, the articles and bloody statutes of Queen Mary repealed.'[15] At the beginning of the eighteenth century John Strype deviated little from this interpretation in his *Annals of the Reformation.* So to all intents and purposes the matter rested until Sir John Neale published the first volume of *Elizabeth I and her Parliaments* in 1953. Rejecting this centuries old consensus he replaced an obstructive House of Lords with a recalcitrant House of Commons, and substituted a conservative for an evangelical queen. Elizabeth, he maintained, wished to reestablish religion as it had been in England in the latter years of her father's reign. Her strategy collapsed because of pressure from the Marian exiles, some like Cooke and Knollys, managing the debates in the Commons, others forming a clerical caucus outside the House. The crown had originally envisaged obtaining an Act of Supremacy in 1559, delaying a full settlement of religion till a later date, but the protestants in the Commons prevented the adoption of this policy of reform of little by little. They forced the queen to extend Parliament after Easter and then to consent to separate Acts of Supremacy and Uniformity. Elizabeth had wanted to move no further than the 1549 Prayer Book which a conservative bishop like Stephen Gardiner had been able to interpret in a catholic sense. The former protestant exiles compelled her to adopt the 1552 Prayer Book to avoid having to make yet greater concessions in a subsequent Parliament.

15 John Foxe, *The Acts and Monuments*, revised and corrected by J. Pratt, VIII (London, 1877), p. 694.

Persuasively argued the Neale thesis proved very influential for many years before it came under critical examination in the early 1980s when two Americans, N. L. Jones and W. S. Hudson, approaching the settlement from rather different positions, advocated a return to the traditional historiographical standpoint. Jones argued that the stubborn resistance of the catholic bishops in the House of Lords put both the queen and the Marian exiles on the defensive early in 1559. He found no evidence of a 'puritan party' in the Commons, and considered that Elizabeth, having with great difficulty overcome the bishops, obtained eventually the settlement she had wanted from the first. W. S. Hudson simultaneously reached a very similar conclusion. Setting the Elizabethan settlement in the context of the Henrician and Edwardian settlements, he demonstrated how the latter led logically to the former. By giving as much emphasis to her chief minister as to the queen he identified circles of acquaintances which went back from Cecil's time as secretary to the Edwardian council to college friendships in late Henrician Cambridge. With Cecil at the centre of the stage previous implausibilities fell into place. An adherent of protestantism, yet a conformist under Mary, Cecil could act as an intermediary between the ultra cautious, politique queen and the Marian exiles, eager for further reform. Cecil, Hudson considered, had abundant justification for his subsequent claim that he had been 'above all others in propagating religion in the beginning of the queen['s reign].'[16]

After the studies of Jones and Hudson it seems unlikely that so much concentration will be paid in the future to the

16 W. S. Hudson, *The Cambridge Connection and the Elizabethan Settlement of 1559* (Durham, North Carolina, 1980), p. 100.

independent actions of the Elizabethan House of Commons, and more stress laid instead upon the plans of Cecil and the queen. The simpler solution may well be preferred to the more complex one. However great the disagreement over the intentions of the main participants in the religious settlement, most historians now would at least concur that the passing of the Acts of Supremacy and Uniformity in May 1559 marked in the country at large not the climax of the English Reformation but only the end of the beginning.

III   The Implementation of the Settlement

Until the queen had formally approved the Acts of Supremacy and Uniformity the government possessed no means of removing recalcitrant catholic clergy from their positions in the church nor of altering the membership of the House of Lords and Convocation. The Act of Supremacy required that 'every archbishop, bishop, and all and every other ecclesiastical person and other ecclesiastical officer and minister...' in addition to 'all and every temporal judge, justicer, mayor and other lay or temporal officer and minister' should take an oath to the queen as the 'only supreme governor of this realm'.[17] The Marian clergy consequently from the early summer of 1559 faced the choice of conforming to a protestant church or of remaining recalcitrant, but at the cost of losing their livings to which protestants could now be preferred. The Act of Uniformity provided that the Prayer Book should come into use on 24 June 1559. Very soon after this date the queen authorised commissions to traverse the country to take oaths from the clergy, remove

17 Elton, *Tudor Constitution*, p. 366.

catholic ornaments from the churches and oversee the enforcement of the new services. Jewel, one such commissioner, in August 1559 sent a letter to Martyr as he was '...on the point of setting out upon a long and troublesome commission for the establishment of religion, through Reading, Abingdon, Gloucester, Bristol, Bath, Wells, Exeter, Cornwall, Dorset and Salisbury. The extent of my journey will be about seven hundred miles, so that I imagine we shall hardly be able to return in less than four months.'[18] Only when the royal commissioners reassembled in London could they discern the magnitude of the task they had undertaken of converting the entire country into a professing protestant nation.

Despite the lead given by the bishops in the Lords in the first Parliament of the reign the government still hoped that some of the Marian episcopate might agree to continue in office in the Elizabethan church. Even as late as September 1559 the queen dispatched a mandate to four catholic bishops to assist at the consecration of Matthew Parker as archbishop of Canterbury. In fact, with the single exception of Anthony Kitchin of Llandaff, all the fourteen surviving Marian bishops refused to take the oath of supremacy and beginning with Edmund Bonner of London between late May and November 1559 all were deprived of their sees. Senior clerics at the universities and members of cathedral chapters showed a similar reluctance to abandon their papal allegiance, demonstrating Cardinal Pole's success in appointing only convinced catholics to vacant posts in the upper reaches of the church. In many cathedrals, as at York, about half the prebendaries chose to surrender their benefices

18 *Zurich Letters*, p. 39.

rather than recognise the queen as the supreme governor of the church, and a significant number of fellows of Oxford and Cambridge Colleges fled to catholic universities on the continent to avoid having to conform. In the parishes matters proceeded very differently with most incumbents continuing in their livings, though, as subsequent events demonstrated, perhaps a majority of these old clergy had little commitment to the new religious settlement.

Uncertainty prevailed throughout the first year of the reign. None of the protestants nominated to the vacant sees could be installed until Parker had formally taken up his duties, and, because of the difficulty in finding sufficient protestant bishops willing to perform the ceremony, his consecration did not take place until 17 December 1559. In consequence for much of the year the initiative rested with the royal commissioners sent out to inspect the church in the regions, and each commission included at least one Marian exile. Besides Jewel, on the commission for the south west of England, Edwin Sandys took part in the visitation of the north of England, Alexander Nowell and Thomas Becon in that of the south and south east, while Nowell for the second time and Thomas Bentham went to the Midlands and Richard Davies and Thomas Young to Wales. Most of the Edwardian protestant bishops, Hooper, Ferrar, Latimer, Ridley and Cranmer himself, had perished in the Marian persecution; on the refusal, therefore, of the catholic bishops to remain in their sees the crown had little choice but to appoint exiles to their offices. Between December 1559 and April 1560 the archbishop consecrated fourteen new bishops to half of the twenty-six sees then vacant in England and Wales, and ten of the fourteen had taken refuge on the continent in the previous reign. Edmund Grindal received the key see of London, Richard Cox Ely, Edwin Sandys Worcester, Nicholas Bullingham Lincoln, James Pilkington Durham, Gilbert Berkley Bath and Wells, Thomas Bentham Coventry and Lichfield, John Parkhurst Norwich, Richard Davies St Asaph and Thomas Young St Davids, which a year later he exchanged for the archbishopric of York. While in theory the queen chose the bishops, all the evidence suggests that at this early period the responsibilities for the appointments rested with Cecil and his closest associates. Whereas the settlement had formally been in force from the time the Acts of Supremacy and Uniformity came into effect, in practice it was only when the new protestant bishops had taken possession of their dioceses that a concerted attempt could be made to impose protestantism upon the nation.

Before Jewel had embarked on his visitation of the west country he had appeared sanguine about the attitudes of the laity towards the settlement. 'The queen is exceedingly well disposed; and the people everywhere thirsting after religion', he had told Martyr in August 1559. On his return to London, however, he sang a different tune: 'It is ... hardly credible what a harvest, or rather what a wilderness of superstition had sprung up in the darkness of the Marian times. We found in all places votive relics of saints, nails with which the infatuated people dreamed that Christ had been pierced, and I know not what small fragments of the sacred cross.'[19]

Most of the Protestant clerics had congregated in London

[19] *Zurich Letters*, pp. 39, 44-5.

after their return from exile and the forwardness of some of the citizens had given them a false impression of the enthusiasm for protestantism in the nation as a whole. From the moment of Elizabeth's accession certain Londoners had exhibited great zeal for reform. Acting on behalf of his fellow Merchant Taylors Richard Hilles, an assiduous correspondent of Bullinger for the previous twenty years, commissioned Richard Mulcaster to write the protestant pageants which greeted the new queen on her entry to the city in January 1559. Although religious conservatism persisted in some parishes, in others citizens had been showing an informed interest in the teachings of the continental reformers since the latter years of Henry VIII's reign. William Bill had preached the protestant gospel at Paul's Cross the Sunday after the queen came to the throne 'to the great delight of the people', some of whom forced their clergy to discontinue the mass without any legal authorization. In St Antholin's and other London parishes wealthy inhabitants were founding lectureships to provide additional preaching and communal psalm singing seems to have gripped the popular imagination. After one little church in London had begun singing in public, Jewel told Martyr early in 1560, the practice had immediately spread to the churches in the neighbourhood and towns much further away. 'You may now sometimes see at Paul's Cross, after the service, six thousand persons, old and young, of both sexes, all singing together and praising God.' In parts of England away from London and the south east some of the laity made their support for a protestant settlement equally evident. Early in the reign some Hull magistrates sent over to Boston in Lincolnshire to secure Melchior Smith for their vicar, and Smith, it emerged a few years later, had been using Calvin's catechism in clandestine teaching in the previous decade. Some of the townspeople, Lever told Bullinger, 'zealous for evangelical truth' had voluntarily raised funds to finance his preaching ministry in Coventry.[20]

Elsewhere in England the laity accepted protestantism far less willingly. If townspeople or local gentry had little appetite for the new uniformity in religion then, apart from the formal change in the liturgy from Latin to English, matters may not at first have appeared so very different from what they had been in catholic times. Stone altars and catholic ornaments remained in more remote churches for many years. The archbishop's visitors discovered in 1567 in the parish church of Wawne in the East Riding of Yorkshire 'pictures of Mary and John with a picture of Christ in the Rood loft, a vestment of fustian with two tunicles of blue for two boys, a superaltar, a Lenten cloth painted with a cross, nails, spears, and such like, a stole, a fanon, the communion table gilded and painted with divers images, the bible torn in certain places, painted pictures of Christopher and others on the church walls...' Even worse at the much more important church of Ripon, where they had 'reserved six great tables of alabaster full of images and forty-nine books, some antiphoners and such books as are condemned by public authority', the vicars had not communicated 'when the communion is ministered in the said church'.[21]

The epidemics of the mid sixteenth century had decimated

20 *Zurich Letters*, pp. 4, 18, 71, 86.
21 J. S. Purvis, *Tudor Parish Documents of the Diocese of York* (Cambridge, 1948), pp. 26-7, 33-4.

the ranks of the lower clergy as well as the episcopate. Few of the surviving parish clergy had undergone an education which would have equipped them to exercise an effective protestant ministry. As Lever explained to Bullinger, 'Many of our parishes have no clergyman, and some dioceses are without a bishop. And out of that very small number who administer the sacraments through this great country, there is hardly one in a hundred who is both able and willing to preach the word of God... Thus indeed is the Lord's harvest very abundant among us, but the labourers are very few.'[22] From the moment they entered into their offices the new bishops turned their attention to reforming Oxford and Cambridge. They succeeded relatively quickly in filling with protestants college posts formerly held by catholics, but it took until the next century for the universities to produce preaching clergy in the numbers a protestant church required.

Professor Collinson has recently remarked that 'by virtue of an authority inherent in their office but effectively delegated from the crown' the first generation of Elizabethan bishops 'promoted a religious policy which was more their own than the crown's and which partly derived from the unofficial Reformation.'[23] The supreme governor, indeed, partly it seems from matters of policy, which the bishops could not or would not understand, partly apparently from personal inclination, demonstrated none of the fervour to evangelise the nation so evident among the former exiles. In April 1559, immediately after the Commons and the Lords had approved the Uniformity Bill, Sandys had understood the proviso

22 *Zurich Letters*, p. 85.
23 P. Collinson, 'The Elizabethan Church and the New Religion', in C. Haigh, ed., *The Reign of Elizabeth*, (London, 1984), p. 177.

retaining ornaments as they had been in the first and second year of the reign of Edward VI to signify 'that we shall not be forced to use them, but that others in the meantime shall not convey them away, but that they may remain for the queen.'[24] Events soon proved how much he had misjudged the situation. In the autumn of 1559 the royal commissioners returned from their visitation of the provinces during which to the best of their abilities they had removed all monuments of superstition from the parish churches only to find that the queen insisted in keeping a 'little silver cross, of ill-omened origin' in her private chapel.[25] As both parties took up entrenched positions it seemed for a time that some of the former exiles would resign their sees rather than stay within a church which as a matter of policy retained catholic ceremonies and ornaments. At this very early period a compromise was effected, the queen kept control over her private chapel while the reformers were not forced to reintroduce the ornaments into the parish churches. With Cecil's help the new bishops won a more decisive victory over the queen in the matter of clerical marriage. When in 1561 Elizabeth attempted to banish clergy wives from colleges and cathedrals, Bishop Cox predicted a clerical exodus with closes abandoned to 'doves and owls ... for any continual housekeeping.'[26] The queen made a partial concession, allowing married clergy to continue to officiate in cathedrals, but from this date until the later nineteenth century in the two universities all senior members of colleges, apart from the master, had to relinquish their fellowships on marriage.

24 *Parker's Correspondence*, p. 65.
25 *Zurich Letters*, p. 55.
26 *Parker's Correspondence*, p. 151.

So from the very beginning there existed this tension between the supreme governor and her episcopate. The bishops strove to convince themselves that they had a 'godly' queen, yet Elizabeth refused to allow protestant considerations to dominate her policy. Whereas she contented herself with outward obedience to the Acts of Supremacy and Uniformity and asked for nothing further, the more forward clergy wanted to bring the entire country to an active commitment to protestantism. The smouldering fire flared anew in 1565 when Elizabeth made a more concerted attempt to enforce a modified form of the ornaments rubric. Perturbed at the lack of uniformity in the matter of clerical dress she commanded Archbishop Parker to ensure that at all services in future as an absolute minimum the surplice should be worn. Although their friends in Zurich counselled conformity, lest by resigning their livings lukewarm clergy should be appointed in their places, some clergy still could not countenance resuming what they saw as the rags of antichrist, and the Vestiarian controversy resulted in almost forty clergy in London alone being suspended from their livings. For the first time, despite the obvious reluctance of most for the task, the queen had forced the reformed bishops to act almost as authoritatively as their catholic predecessors. In London the deprivations provoked popular unrest, and Grindal wrote anxiously to Cecil to relate how, after he had suspended 'one Bartlett, a reader of a divinity lecture in St Giles' parish without Cripplegate', 'three-score women' had come to his house to make suit for him, and only the intervention of another deprived minister, Mr Philpot, had persuaded them to go away.[27]

27 W. Nicholson, ed., *The Remains of Edmund Grindal* (Parker Society, Cambridge, 1843), pp. 288-9.

The queen's attempt to obtain an outward uniformity in liturgical dress brought the first open splintering of the protestant ranks when a group of Londoners decided to set up a separate church of their own. This horrified Grindal who believed that 'in this severing yourselves from the society of other christians, you condemn not only us, but also the whole state of the church reformed in King Edward's days, which was well reformed according to the word of God, yea, and many good men have shed their blood for the same.' In vindication of their actions the dissenters replied that when the bishops displaced their preachers for not subscribing to their apparel and began prosecuting the laity for not going to their parish churches 'we bethought us what were best to do; and we remembered that there was a congregation of us in this city in Queen Mary's days; and a congregation at Geneva, which used a book and order of preaching, ministering of sacraments and discipline, most agreeable to the word of God; ... which book and order we now hold.'[28] A theological justification of separatism did not emerge until the writings of Robert Browne and Robert Harrison some fifteen years later, but this practical demonstration of the potential of radical protestantism to endanger religious unity deeply troubled both the defenders of the settlement and those striving for further reform.

The Vestiarian controversy not only led to isolated instances of separatism in London and later in Cambridge and Norwich but also, much more significantly, materially contributed to the development of presbyterianism. Discontent in London over the ejection of the nonconforming ministers caused a group of Londoners based on the Minories also to

28 *op. cit.*, pp. 202, 203-4.

look to the practice of the church of Geneva, but these clergy and laity, unlike the separatists confronting Grindal, were aiming at nothing less than a fully reformed church which included the entire nation. In this presbyterian church, organised from the parishes upwards and not as then pertained from the crown and episcopate downwards, bishops would have no role at all and the supreme governor enjoy no greater powers than any other lay person. These Londoners, very effectively organised by John Field, in 1570 found their intellectual leader in Thomas Cartwright, who in his Cambridge lectures on the Acts of the Apostles, set out the blueprint of an English presbyterian church.

At the time of the Vestiarian controversy many of the bishops had sympathised with the nonconformists, for they, too, considered that Romish vestments did not make for edification in a rightly reformed church, and only wore them for obedience sake. When in 1570, however, the whole system of church government came under attack, they reacted very differently and to a man rallied to the queen and the civil government, condemning those who, as *The Admonition to the Parliament* of 1572 made plain, had as their object 'to revive the ancient presbytery of the primitive church, and to establish such an equality among all ministers, that they may be despised and rejected even by the church itself.'[29]

So within a decade of the passing of the Acts of Supremacy and Uniformity it had become clear that the settlement of religion had not proved acceptable to certain committed protestants to whom their enemies were just beginning to

29 *Zurich Letters*, p. 285.

refer as puritans. As the pamphlet contest between Thomas Cartwright and John Whitgift demonstrated in the 1570s, presbyterianism appears always to have been a clerically dominated movement without a substantial popular base, while separatism, though it attracted lay participation, remained numerically extremely small. Whatever their reservations, most convinced protestants continued to work within the structures of the established church. Particularly in the south and south east many towns funded lectureships out of their own resources to obtain regular courses of sermons which so may parish incumbents could still not provide. As time progressed this constant preaching in certain towns did seem to be in the process of creating a godly urban elite, though these protestants continued to complain that the harvest was plenteous and the labourers few.

Conversion of the masses to real as opposed to nominal protestantism took a very long time and may never have affected other than a minority of the population. Many more Elizabethans may have adopted protestantism for negative rather than positive reasons. Between 1558 and 1603 attitudes towards catholicism changed fundamentally, the majority of the nation ceasing to regard it any longer as the 'old religion' but seeing it instead as foreign, unEnglish and even antichristian. 1570 witnessed a sea change. Restrained by Philip II the pope took no public action when Parliament renounced the papal supremacy in 1559. After their ejection from their sees Marian bishops similarly gave no lead to the English laity. Some catholic intellectuals, unwilling to recognise the queen's authority in the church, went into exile on the continent and mounted a propaganda campaign against the new regime. It seems, however, that in the first and crucial decade of the reign the laity inclined towards catholicism with varying degrees of reluctance continued to attend church Sunday by Sunday, and the government's hope that the tenets of the Prayer Book might be being absorbed by a process of osmosis appeared to be being achieved. Two events, the foundation in 1568 by William Allen of an English catholic college at Douai and the northern rebellion in the autumn of 1569 totally altered the situation within a very short space of time. While it would appear that the earls of Northumberland, Cumberland and Westmorland had recourse to arms primarily because of their discontent over their exclusion from political power, they used religion to give credibility to their actions. When their forces captured Durham, catholic priests once again said mass openly in the cathedral which for the previous decade Dean Whittingham had been attempting to turn into a protestant citadel. Government troops fairly quickly overcame the rebels, the rising gained nothing like the support in the region the Pilgrimage of Grace had done some thirty years previously, but this news took time to reach Rome. In a bull dated April 1570 Pius V accused Elizabeth I of 'having seized the crown and monstrously usurped the place of supreme head of the church in all England, together with the chief authority and jurisdiction belonging to it,' and reducing 'this same kingdom, which had already been restored to the catholic faith and to good fruits, to a miserable ruin.' Having then detailed how the mass had been overthrown, catholic priests deprived and 'impious rites and institutions after the rule of Calvin' brought in, he declared the queen 'to be deprived of her pretended title to the aforesaid crown and of all lordship, dignity and privilege whatsoever; and also the nobles, subjects and people of the said realm, and all others who have in any way sworn oaths to her, to be for ever absolved from such an oath and from any duty arising from lordship, fealty and obedience.[30]

Even though, once he had heard of the failure of the rebellion, the pope withheld the execution of the bull until a more propitious time, the excommunication of the queen threw the protestant governing classes into an understandable panic. Only the life of Elizabeth stood between them and the restoration of catholicism. A clamorous group in both the Lords and Commons would have liked to have compelled all inhabitants not only to attend church every week as had been established by the Act of Uniformity, but now also to receive the protestant communion at Easter. The queen would not countenance this demand, but the 1571 Act against bringing in and putting in execution of bulls and other instruments from the see of Rome condemned as traitors those who broke the law, and the penalty of treason was death.

The promulgation of the papal bull increased the fervour of the young Englishmen who had chosen to seek a catholic education at the English college at Douai. At first Allen seems to have intended the institution primarily as a means of defending the faith by literary means, but it speedily became a seminary for the conversion of the nation. The first

30 Elton, *Tudor Constitution*, pp. 416-18.

Douai educated priests entered the country in 1574 and from that date for the remainder of the reign these seminary priests, joined later by the first English Jesuits, embarked on the enterprise of England. Ever since Elizabeth's accession some noble, gentry and professional families had consciously separated themselves from the heretical church; the new seminary priests from the 1570s onwards insisted that catholics should in no way conform to the established religion and won numbers of erstwhile church papists back to Rome. Particularly in the north of England recusancy became a major problem for both the civil and ecclesiastical authorities. Probably most of the priests coming into the country concentrated upon winning souls for the Roman church, but from the time that the head of that church had pronounced Elizabeth not to be the legal queen of England, religion and politics could no longer be divided. Abroad English priests like Robert Parson were definitely scheming to secure a catholic successor to Elizabeth, if not to procure her death, and until 1587 they had a catholic candidate to hand in Mary Queen of Scots. Resentment at intrusion by a foreign power in the internal affairs of England, and loyalty to the last of the Tudors played an ever greater part in uniting the country behind Elizabeth. Cecil appealed to this element of nationalism in 1583 when he published his *Execution of Justice in England.* Throughout his tract he maintained there had been no persecution for religion since 1558; the queen and parliament had proceeded as any other state would have done against the 'seedmen of sedition' who 'have enticed and sought to persuade by their secret false reasons the people to allow and believe all the actions and attempts whatsoever the pope hath done or shall do to be lawful...' The state, he contended, had taken justifiable action against the priests because 'they have reconciled and withdrawn so many people in corners from the laws of the realm to the obedience of the pope, a foreign potentate and open enemy, whom they know to have already declared the queen to be no lawful queen, to have maintained the known rebels and traitors, to have invaded her majesty's dominions with open war.'[31]

Perceptions of catholics, especially of catholic priests in general and Jesuits in particular, created by this sort of propaganda may have contributed as much as, if not more than the sermons of protestant preachers to changing England into a protestant country. The process extended over many decades, and the ideal may have been never achieved, but the spontaneous celebration of the queen's accession day together with, from the early seventeenth century, the equally enthusiastic symbolic burning of Guy Fawkes suggest that England had at least become a virulently anticatholic nation.

In the last years of his life Archbishop Parker confided to Cecil his concern over the permanence of the religious settlement. The English catholics buoyed up by the massacre of protestants in Paris on St Bartholomew's day, seemed 'marvellous bold'. 'If that only desperate person [Mary Queen of Scots] were away, as by justice soon it might be,' he observed in 1572, 'the queen's majesty's good subjects would be in better hope, and the papists' daily expectation vanquished.' On the other flank he feared the danger pre-

31 R. M. Kingdon, ed., *'The Execution of Justice in England'* by *William Cecil, and 'A Truce, Sincere and Modest Defense of English Catholics' by William Cecil* (Cornell University Press, Ithaca, New York, 1965), p. 37.

sented by the presbyterians and separatists, with the dreadful social experiment of the anabaptists at Munster never far from his mind. 'The comfort that these puritans have, and their continuance, is marvellous', he complained some months later, 'and therefore, if her highness with her council (I mean some of them) step not to it, I see the likelihood of a pitiful commonwealth to follow...' The queen, he asserted in his last letter, was 'in constancy almost alone to be offended with the puritans, whose government in conclusion will undo her and all others that depend upon her her'... 'Does your lordship think that I care either for cap, tippet, surplice, or wafer-bread or any such? But for the laws so established I esteem them...'. Parker died in the spring of 1575, a disillusioned old man, apprehensive of what the future might hold for Elizabeth and her church. He ought to have had more confidence in the queen's determination 'princely to govern' and in Cecil's support for the royal supremacy and for uniformity in religion.[32] The partnership between the supreme governor and her chief minister lasted a further twenty years and largely through their efforts in the second half of the sixteenth century the religious settlement survived without substantial change until the Civil War.

<hr/>

32 *Parker's Correspondence*, pp. 399, 418, 478-9.

in England, Henry VIII to James I, (London, 1977); R. O'Day and F. Heal, *Princes and Paupers in the English Church, 1500-1800* (Leicester, 1981) and P. Lake and M. Dowling, eds., *Protestantism and the National Church in Sixteenth Century England* (London, 1987). The classic study of Elizabethan Presbyterianism is by P. Collinson, *The Elizabethan Puritan Movement* (London, 1967). Particularly illuminating are two of his later books, P. Collinson, *The Religion of Protestants: The Church in English Society 1559-1625* (Oxford, 1982) and P. Collinson, *The Birthpangs of Protestant England: Religious and Cultural Change in the Sixteenth and Seventeenth Centuries* (London, 1988). The best study of Elizabethan Separatism is B. R. White, *The English Separatism Tradition* (Oxford, 1971). In *Anglicans and Puritans? Presbyterianism and English Conformist Thought from Whitgift to Hooker* (London, 1988) P. Lake has clarified differences between Presbyterians and the defenders of the established church. The most detailed history of Elizabethan Catholicism is still A. O. Meyer, *England and the Catholic Church under Queen Elizabeth* (English edition, London, 1915, re-issue 1967). Two studies, J. Bossy, *The English Catholic Community 1570-1850* (London, 1975) and J. C. H. Aveling, *The Handle and the Axe: the Catholic Recusants in England from Reformation to Emancipation* (London, 1976), suggest that English Catholicism had a new beginning in 1570, an interpretation which is attacked by C. Haigh in, among other places, 'The Continuity of Catholicism in the English Reformation', in C. Haigh, ed., *The English Reformation Revised* (Cambridge, 1987) and 'The Church of England, the Catholics and the People', in C. Haigh, ed., *The Reign of Elizabeth I* (London, 1984). Three particularly good studies illustrate the diversity of religious adherence in different regions in the Elizabethan period: C. Haigh, *Reformation and Resistance in Tudor Lancashire* (Cambridge, 1975), D. MacCulloch, *Suffolk and the Tudors* (Oxford, 1986) and S. Brigden, *London and the Reformation* (Oxford, 1989).

Bibliography of Claire Cross

1953
The Free Grammar School of Leicester, Leicester University Press, 1953, pp. 51.

1960
'Noble Patronage in the Elizabethan Church', *Historical Journal*, III, 1960, pp. 16.

1961
'An Exchange of Lands with the Crown', *Bulletin of the Institute of Historical Research*, XXXIV, 1961, pp. 5.

1962
'The Third Earl of Huntingdon and Elizabethan Leicestershire', *Transactions of the Leicestershire Archaeological and Historical Society*, XXXVI, 1962, pp. 15.

1963
'Berwick on Tweed and the Neighbouring Parts of Northumberland on the Eve of the Armada', *Archaeologia Aeliana*, 4th Series, XLI, 1963, pp. 11.

1964
'The Hastings Manuscripts: Sources for Leicestershire History in California', *Transactions of the Leicestershire Archaeological and Historical Society*, XXXVIII, 1964, pp. 13.

1965

'The Third Earl of Huntingdon and the Trials of Catholics in the North', *Recusant History*, VIII, 1965, pp. 10.
'An Example of Lay Intervention in the Elizabethan Church', *Studies in Church History*, II, 1965, pp. 10.

1966

The Puritan Earl: The Life of Henry Hastings, Third Earl of Huntingdon, 1536-1595, Macmillan, 1966, pp. 372.

1967

'Supervising the Finances of the Third Earl of Huntingdon, 1580-1595', *Bulletin of the Institute of Historical Research,* XL, 1967, pp. 15.
'Achieving the Millennium: the Church in York during the Commonwealth', *Studies in Church History*, IV, 1967, pp. 20.

1969

The Royal Supremacy in the Elizabethan Church, Allen and Unwin, 1969, pp. 239.
The Letters of Sir Francis Hastings, 1574-1609, Somerset Record Society, 1969, pp. 141.

1970

'The Economic Problems of the See of York; Decline and Recovery in the Sixteenth Century' in J. Thirsk, ed., *Land, Church and People: Essays presented to Professor H.P.R. Finberg*, Agricultural History Review, vol. XVIII, Supplement, 1970, pp. 17.

1971

'"He-Goats before the Flocks"; A Note on the Part played by Women in the Founding of some Civil War Churches', *Studies in Church History*, VIII, 1971, pp. 7.

1972

'The Church in England 1646-1660', in G.E. Aylmer, ed., *The Interregnum: The Quest for Settlement 1646-1660*, Macmillan, 1972, pp. 21.

'"Dens of Loitering Lubbers": Protestant Protest against Cathedral Foundations', *Studies in Church History*, IX, 1972, pp. 8.

1975

'Popular Piety and the Records of the Unestablished Churches 1460-1660', *Studies in Church History*, XI, 1975 pp. 23.

1976

Church and People 1450-1660: The Triumph of the Laity in the English Church, Fontana, 1976, pp. 273.

1977

'Churchmen and the Royal Supremacy', in F. Heal and R. O'Day, eds., *Church and Society in England: Henry VIII to James I*, Macmillan, 1977, pp. 20.

'From the Reformation to the Restoration', in G.E. Aylmer and R. Cant, eds., *A History of York Minster*, Oxford, 1977, pp. 30

'Les Difficultés soulevées par les Institutions Non-reformées de l'Église face au progrès du Protestantism dans L'Angleterre du XVIeme Siècle', in M. Peronnet, ed., *Les Églises et leurs Institutions au XVIeme Siècle*, Montpellier,

1977, pp. 18.

1978

"Great Reasoners in Scripture": The Activities of Women Lollards', in D. Baker, ed., *Medieval Women: Essays Presented to Professor R.M.T. Hill*, Studies in Church History, Subsidia I, 1978, pp. 21.

'York Clerical Piety and St Peter's School on the Eve of the Reformation', *York Historian*, II, 1978, pp. 4.

1979

'Continental Students and the Protestant Reformation in England in the Sixteenth Century', in D. Baker, ed., *Reform and Reformation: England and the Continent c 1500-c 1750: Essays presented to Professor C.W. Dugmore*, Studies in Church History, Subsidia II, 1979, pp. 23.

'Religious and Social Protest among Lollards in Early Tudor England', in *The Church in a Changing Society*, C.H.I.E.C. Conference Proceedings, Uppsala, 1979, pp. 5.

'Parochial Structure and the Dissemination of Protestantism in Sixteenth Century England: A Tale of Two Cities', *Studies in Church History*, XVI, 1979, pp. 10.

'From Estate to Profession: The Transformation of the English Clergy in the Sixteenth and early Seventeenth Century', in P. Butel, ed., *Sociétés et Groupes Socieux en Aquitaine et en Angleterre*, Bordeaux, 1979, pp. 8.

1980

'Priests into Ministers: The Establishment of Protestant Practice in the City of York, 1530-1630', in P.N. Brooks, ed., *Reformation Principle and Practice: Essays in Honour of Professor A.G. Dickens*, Scolar Press, 1980, pp. 21.

44

'Irenical Tendencies in the Elizabethan Church', *Nederlands Archief voor Kerkgeschiedenis*, LX, 1980, pp. 7.

'Lay Literacy and Clerical Misconduct in a York parish during the Reign of Mary Tudor', *York Historian*, III, 1980, pp. 6.

'La Suprématie Royale et les Controverses Religieuses en Angleterre sous le Regne d'Elisabeth I', in M. Peronnet, ed., *La Controverse Religieuse*, Montpellier, 1980, pp. 8.

1981

'The Incomes of Provincial Urban Clergy, 1520-1645', in R. O'Day and F. Heal, eds., *Princes and Paupers in the English Church*, Leicester University Press, 1981, pp. 25.

'The State and the Development of Protestantism in English Towns, 1520-1603', in A.C. Duke and C.A. Tamse, eds., *Britain and the Netherlands*, VII, The Hague, 1981, pp. 23.

1982

'Dynastic Politics: The Local and National Importance of the Hastings Family in the Sixteenth Century', in M. Palmer, ed., *The Aristocratic Estate: The Hastings in Leicestershire and South Derbyshire*, Loughborough University, 1982, pp. 19.

'The Development of Protestantism in Leeds and Hull, 1520-1640: The Evidence from Wills', *Northern History*, XVIII, 1982, pp. 10.

1984

York Clergy Wills 1520-1600: 1 The Minster Clergy, Borthwick Texts and Calendars: Records of the Northern Province, 10, University of York, 1984, pp. 179.

'Wills as Evidence of Popular Piety in the Reformation

Period: Leeds and Hull 1540-1640', in D. Loades, ed., *The End of Strife: Death, Reconciliation and Expressions of Christian Spirituality*, Edinburgh, 1984, pp. 8.

1985

Urban Magistrates and Ministers: Religion in Hull and Leeds from the Reformation to the Civil War, Borthwick Paper, York, 1985, pp. 29.

'The Third Earl of Huntingdon's Death-bed: a Calvinist Example of the Ars Moriendi', *Northern History*, XXI, 1985, pp. 28.

1986

'Oxford and the Tudor State from the Accession of Henry VIII to the Death of Mary', in J. McConica, ed., *The History of the University of Oxford, volume III: The Collegiate University*, Oxford, 1986, pp. 33.

'The Genesis of a Godly Community: Two York Parishes, 1590-1640', *Studies in Church History*, 23, 1986, pp. 14.

1987

'Northern Women in the Early Modern Period: the Female Testators of Hull and Leeds 1520-1650', *Journal of the Yorkshire Archaeological Society*, 59, 1987, pp. 12.

'Protestant Attitudes towards Episcopacy in the Early Elizabethan Church', *Miscellanea Historiae Ecclesiasticae*, VIII, Louvain, 1987, pp. 8.

1988

C. Cross, D. Loades and J. J. Scarisbrick, eds., *Law and Government under the Tudors: Essays presented to Sir Geoffrey Elton on his Retirement*, Cambridge, 1988, pp.

275.

'Sin and Society: the Northern High Commission and the Northern Gentry in the Reign of Elizabeth I', in C. Cross, D. Loades and J. J. Scarisbrick, eds., *Law and Government under the Tudors*, Cambridge, 1988, pp. 15.

'The English Church on the Eve of the Reformation', *History Sixth*, II, 1988, pp. 5.

'Monasticism and Society in the Diocese of York 1520-1540', *Transactions of the Royal Historical Society*, 38, 1988, pp. 15.

1989

'Les couvents de femmes et la societé laïque dans le nord de l'Angleterre à la veille de la Réforme', in *Vie Ecclésiale, Communauté et Communautés*, Universite Paris - Val-de-Marne, Groupe de Recherches sur l'Histoire et la Pensee Religieuses Anglaises, Didier-Erudition, Paris, 1989, pp. 15.

York Clergy Wills 1520-1600: 2. The City Clergy, Borthwick Texts and Calendars: Records of the Northern Province 15, York, 1989, pp. 126.

'A Medieval Yorkshire Library', *Northern History*, 25, 1989, pp. 10.

'A Metamorphosis of Ministry: Former Yorkshire Monks and Friars in the Sixteenth-Century English Protestant Church', *Journal of the United Reformed Church History Society*, 4 no 5, 1989 pp. 16.

1990

'"I was a Stranger, and Ye took Me in": Polish Religious Refugees in England and English Refugees in Poland in the Sixteenth Century', *Studies in Church History*, Subsidia 6,

Oxford, 1990 pp. 8.
'Community Solidarity among Yorkshire Religious after the Dissolution', in J. Loades, ed., *Monastic Studies: the Continuity of Tradition*, I, Bangor, 1990 pp. 10.
'The Religious Life of Women in Sixteenth Century Yorkshire', *Studies in Church History*, 27, Oxford, 1990 pp. 18.
'Communal Piety in Sixteenth Century Boston', *Lincolnshire History and Archaeology*, 25, 1990 pp. 6.

1991
'Conflict and Confrontation: the York Dean and Chapter and the Corporation in the 1630s', in D. Marcombe and C. S. Knighton, eds., *Close Encounters: English Cathedrals and Society since 1549*, Nottingham, 1991, pp. 10.
'Monks and Learning in Sixteenth Century Yorkshire', *Studies in Church History*, Subsidia 8, Oxford, 1991, pp. 15.
'Monks, Friars and the Royal Supremacy in Sixteenth Century Yorkshire' *Studies in Church History*, Subsidia 9, Oxford, 1991 pp. 20.

Forthcoming
'A Man of Conscience in Seventeenth-Century Urban Politics: Alderman Hoyle of York', in J. Morrill, P. Slack and D. Woolf, eds., *Public Duty and Private Conscience: Essays in Honour of Gerald Aylmer*, 1993
'Orthodoxy and Heterodoxy in the English Reformation: the Married Yorkshire Religious', in *Orthodoxie et Herésie*, Université Paris - Val-de-Marne, Groupe de Recherches sur l'Histoire et la Pensee religieuses anglaises, Didier-Erudition, Paris

C. Cross and N. Vickers, eds., *Yorkshire Religious in the Sixteenth Century*, Yorkshire Archaeological Society, Record Series

'The Reconstitution of Northern Monastic Communities in the Reign of Mary Tudor', *Northern History*

'An Elizabethan Martyrologist and his Martyr; John Mush and Margaret Clitherow', *Studies in Church History*, 30

'No Continuing City: English Protestant Exiles and Continental Protestant Refugees in the English Reformation 1520-1570', The Reformation

The End of Medieval Monasticism in the East Riding of Yorkshire, East Yorkshire Local History Society